D0982908

INDIAN FISHING AND CAMPING

G.W.

INDIAN FISHING AND CAMPING

WRITTEN AND ILLUSTRATED BY

ROBERT HOFSINDE
(GRAY-WOLF)

WILLIAM MORROW & CO.
NEW YORK 1963

By the Same Author:

THE INDIAN AND THE BUFFALO

THE INDIAN AND HIS HORSE

INDIAN BEADWORK

INDIAN GAMES AND CRAFTS

INDIAN HUNTING

INDIAN PICTURE WRITING

INDIAN SIGN LANGUAGE

THE INDIAN'S SECRET WORLD

Published simultaneously in the Dominion of
Canada by George J. McLeod Limited, Toronto.
Printed in the United States of America.
Library of Congress Catalog Card Number 63-8798

To Obed May,
friend and nature lover.

CONTENTS

INDIAN FISHING AND CAMPING

G.W.

1

Fishing and Camping

WE estimate today that fish of some kind have been on earth for about 360 million years, while man, a latecomer, appeared around 2 million years ago. Acquiring food was his most important activity, and he soon learned to fish, taking his catch by hand from shallow streams and pools. As time passed he learned how to make nets and spears, and fishing for food became easier.

Next in importance to feeding himself, early

man had to find or make shelter of some kind against rain and sun, cold and snow. He was a camper, not from choice, but from necessity. Later, when he discovered fire, he was able to keep his camps warm, to cook his food, and to protect himself against night-roaming animals. Slowly his shelter improved and it became portable.

The Indians were camping long before the Europeans came to America. Some of them had permanent villages. Others, such as the Plains Indians, moved their camps as they followed the buffalo. The woodland Indians made their camps throughout the forests, as they gathered berries and maple sap or went fishing.

These early camps were not like the vacation camps we know today, but were places where work had to be done constantly. Canoes needed patching; a new paddle was required; buckskin clothing had to be mended; and other seemingly endless tasks had to be performed. Camping was still hard work when Lewis and Clark and the men of their expedition explored the West from 1804 to 1806. Night after night, wherever the end of the

day found them, they set up camp, checked over their equipment, cooked their rations, and slept—often in a pouring rain. Shelters and sleeping bags were unknown. They had no portable stoves or lanterns. In fact, each man's gear was held to a minimum.

The Canadian *voyageurs* also camped at night along their watery highways. We can be sure that they slept well, for according to some of their old journals, their day started at 2:30 in the morning and ended at 8:00 in the evening, with only a rest now and again for "a pipe." Trappers and mountain men lived in cabins, but often they too found themselves camping on the trail when the sun went down.

There is romance in the word *camping*. Growing from a necessity of daily life, it has become a wonderful form of recreation. Today, with modern and improved camping gear and with a car for transportation, we can go for health and fun to public camp sites in our national and state forests and in the provinces of Canada.

Whenever we camp out or build a summer cottage or cabin, we seek a spot for its beauty and solitude. And if we venture into the areas designated as wilderness, where nature is unspoiled, we can still see the country as the Indian saw it. But no matter what type of camping trip we go on, whether it is for the week end or for the summer, close to home or in another state, the camp will usually be set up near a lake or river. And that calls for fishing. At such times you might like to fish as the Indians did and with the same gear that they made and used.

2

Fishing the Indian Way

PRIMITIVE man did not fish for sport. To him, both fishing and hunting were essential in the grim, constant struggle for survival.

The American Indian also fished to add to his food supply. And as the population increased and families banded together for protection in camps and villages, he needed more food and, in turn, more fish. In addition to spearing their catch, the Indians developed other faster and more efficient ways of fishing, making use of lines, hooks, lures, and sinkers. They learned to make this fishing equipment from the many things nature had to offer them. In the woods plant fibers served as material for nets, traps, and weirs. On the treeless plains they used animal hides and sinew instead.

Since trees, roots, and nettles were abundant on the Pacific Coast, the Indians living there—and the woodland tribes inland—used spruce root, vegetable fiber, especially from nettle, and the inner bark of some trees to make cordage for their nets. In the coastal area they usually took bark from the great white cedars.

A Pacific Coast Indian obtained his cordage material by making a slashing cut in the bark close to the base of a tree. Then, with an upward pull, he stripped off the longest piece possible. After that, the strips were soaked in water, usually in a running stream, so they would become pliable. This treatment made it easy to separate the inner and outer sections.

The Indian then split the inner bark into long ribbons of the sizes needed by running his thumb-

G.
W.
SPLICE.
ROLLING.

nail down the strip. To give these bark strips even more strength and pliability, he boiled them in a lye mixture, made from water and wood ashes. The strips were hung over a smooth pole to dry and then pulled back and forth on it, which caused the bark to split again into threadlike strands.

Next he placed two strands side by side on his upper thigh and rolled them toward his knee with his flat, open palm until they were twisted into one, heavier strand. To make the cord longer, he shortened one strand, laid the end of a new strand next to its end, and continued rolling it with the longer strand of the original cord. This longer strand now became the shorter, and the same process was repeated with it. In this manner he spliced the ends so they held firmly. The finished cord was used for fishlines and for nets.

These Indians often set up their nets in rivers, suspending them from poles that were placed from shore to shore on the sandy bottom. As the fish tried to swim through the nets, they were caught by the gills, thus giving the nets the name of gill nets.

At other times the Indians pulled a fish net between two canoes as they slowly paddled up a river. To keep the bottom of the net down, they weighted it with stones, which were sometimes tied up in small buckskin bags. There were two men in each canoe; one handled the net, while his companion paddled. As more and more fish became enmeshed, the net began to drag heavily, and the paddlers began to paddle harder and faster. As they moved forward, they brought the canoes together. This closed the open ends of the net and prevented the fish from escaping when the net was pulled aboard or onshore.

Large long-handled nets, which were held open with great hoops, were used on the Columbia River in Oregon. Standing on wooden platforms that extended from the rocks, out over the boiling waters, the Indians were able to scoop up leaping salmon with these nets when they swam upriver to spawn.

Always alert to the ways of the natural world, all Indians observed everything closely. This was part of their schooling, and they learned their

GRAY-
WOLF.

lessons well. An Ojibwa Indian learned that where eddies swirled around boulders in a stream, he would find whitefish. These he caught from his canoe with a smaller type of scoop net. The scoop net was sometimes round, sometimes triangular, and it was much in use among these Indians when they fished the inland streams.

When going after whitefish, one Ojibwa paddled from the stern while another lowered his net gently into the water from the bow of the canoe. He held the net there until its weight told him that he had caught a fish. Then he gave the net a deft twist and hauled it close to the canoe. A man had to be an expert not to upset the canoe when he pulled up such a fighting fish, weighing from two to fifteen pounds.

The whitefish season lasted from May until November, and during those months the Ojibwa Indians fished for them constantly. Like the cod, the whitefish cured well. Cut open, cleaned, and spread out to dry, it kept for many months.

The Indians always cleaned their fish as soon as possible to keep them from spoiling. When the fishing camp was a long way from the main village, it was an advantage to dry and smoke the catch at once, making it lighter to transport home. This was especially important when there were long portages to be made.

The bark strips the Northwest tribes made into twine for their nets were also used to make rope for their large fish traps. Cutting the strands about half as thick as he wanted the finished rope to be, the Indian looped two of them over a stout peg, set in the ground, and knotted them together close to the peg. There were then four strands leading from the knot. The two strands on the ropemaker's right were twisted together with a right-hand turn. The left-hand strands were also twisted together to the right. This left the ropemaker with two rolled strands instead of four loose ones. Now the two were twisted into one, with the worker making the turns to his left. Additional strands were spliced to the ends during the making, just as in adding to the twine. Such a rope did not come apart.

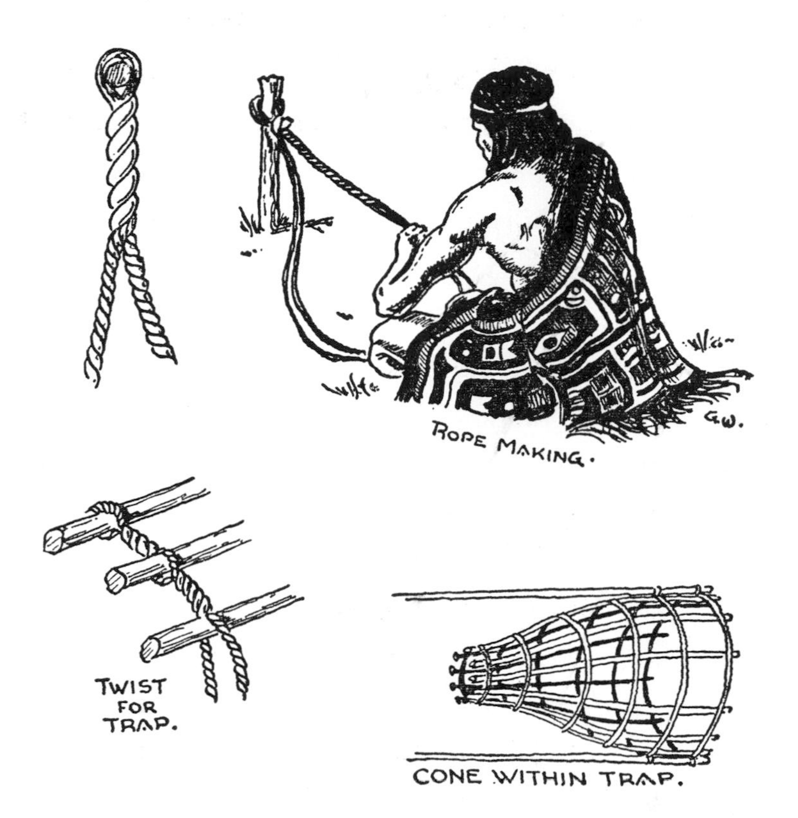

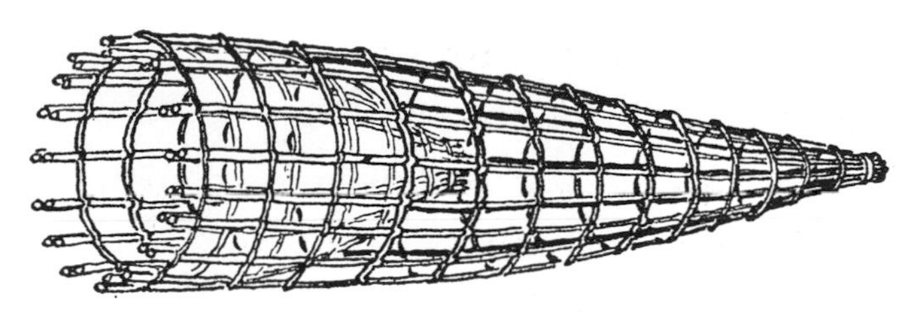

FINISHED TRAP

The fish traps were held together with this rope. They were made from long willow poles in the shape of very deep baskets. Starting with one pole, the Indian tied a rope to one end of it and then twisted it in left-hand turns for a distance of three to four inches. At this point another pole was pushed through the strands and a few more turns taken in the rope. This continued until the poles were arranged in a circle of the proper size, with loops of rope connecting them.

A foot or so below the first circle of rope another circle was added to the poles. This was repeated until the willows were held together from end to end. However, as each circle of rope was twisted into position the willows were pulled closer and closer together, so that the trap gradually tapered to a point at the end in the form of a cone.

Next a shorter cone, held together in the same manner, was made from thinner willows. Instead of closing the tapered end completely, however, the fisherman left the second cone open like a funnel. The small cone was placed inside the large cone, and the broad openings of each were tied together. The finished trap was then placed in a stream, anchored down, and set, so that the opening faced upstream. When fish entered the trap, many of them swam through the funnel, and then could not get out again.

The Indians made daily visits to these traps, and when they were filled with fish they were hauled onshore. A fisherman opened the pointed end of his trap and poured the catch into storage boxes or baskets. Then he closed the traps and reset them.

When fishing for sturgeon, the woodland Indians preferred to use spears, because this game fish is very hard to take with hook and line. It often reaches a length of 7 feet and a weight of 275 pounds, and one good catch fed an Indian family for a long time.

At the height of the fishing season, the Indians often fished for sturgeon at night. Adding two slender poles to their canoes and placing them so they extended well out in front, they hung a bark box between them. The box was filled with

GRDN. WOLF.

sand, into which a pine-knot torch was firmly set. The spearman then fastened a birch-bark shield across the poles between the box and the canoe. It kept the light out of his eyes when the torch was lit. Once it became dark the flame of the torch lured the fish within reach of the spear. In this manner the Indians caught many a great sturgeon, whitefish, trout, and pike, and provided winter food for their people.

Although the Indians usually fished with gear we still use today, such as hooks, nets, spears, and traps, they also caught fish in ways that were unique. Sometimes an Indian lay down on a log that had fallen into a stream. When a trout came to the log, he put his right arm into the water, slowly reached up, and tickled the trout's belly. The fish remained motionless all the while until, suddenly, the Indian grasped it quickly and brought it out of the water.

The Pacific Coast tribes invented an odd piece of fishing equipment that looked like a rake. It was made from a long, flat cedar board, into which was set a row of sharp bones, all pointing forward.

In the center of the board the Indians inserted a long handle or, if the rake was very wide, they attached a handle at each end. They dragged this rakelike instrument along the sandy bottom of a fairly shallow stream until a number of herring were impaled on the bone points.

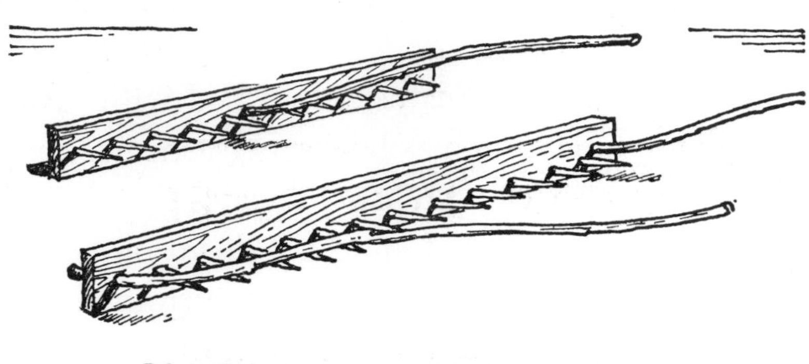

PACIFIC COAST HERRING RAKES

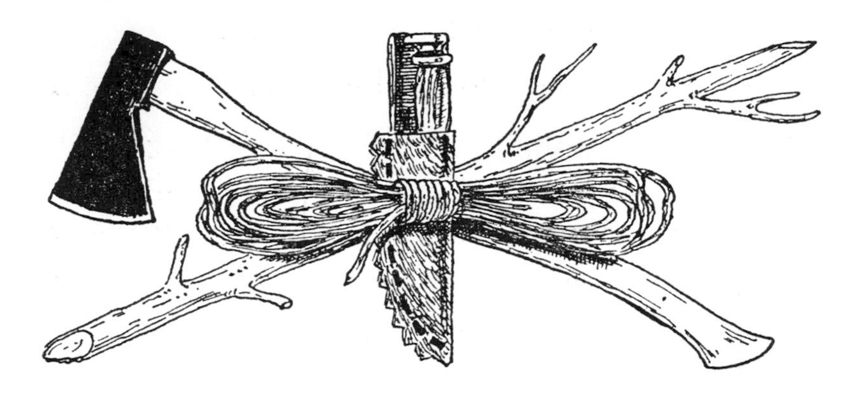

3

Make Your Gear

MANY a fish has been caught with such simple equipment as a pole, a string, and a bent pin. Some of the Indian gear is as easy to make and to use, and it will probably give you better results. If you and your father are on a week-end camping trip, but you have no fishing gear, then why not try fishing the Indian way?

The simplest tackle you can begin with is a hook, line, and sinker. A flexible willow rod or the trunk of a young sapling will serve as a fishing pole, and it need not be over five feet long.

It is better to use hardwood than softwood when making the rest of your equipment. Although it is a little more difficult to work with, your finished gear will last longer. Among the hardwoods are hickory, oak, beech, sugar maple, birch, and locust. In the South you will find live oak and ironwood, as well as the white and the post oak.

The easiest hook to make is the gorge hook. Whittle a two- to three-inch hardwood twig until it is pointed sharply at both ends. In the center of the twig, cut a shallow groove to hold the line. (See figure A.) Take care that this cut is not too deep, or the hook will break when you try to land

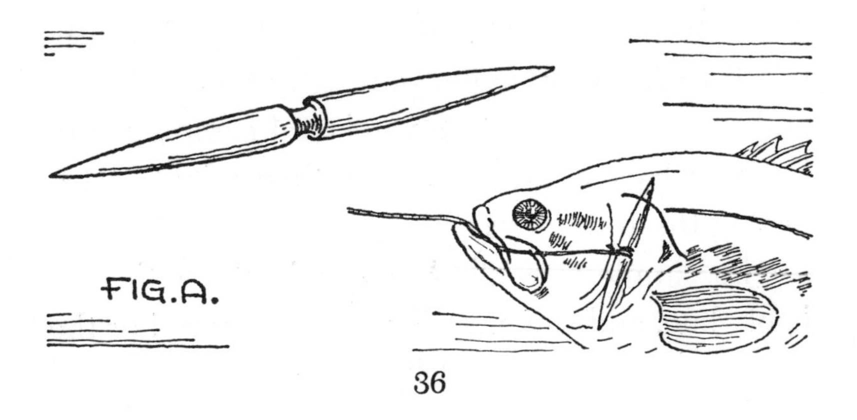

a fish. After you tie the hook to your line, cover it completely with bait, either suet or worms. When the fish takes the bait, it will swallow the entire hook. As it tries to swim away with it, the hook will set itself crosswise in either its mouth or its stomach.

Another type of wooden hook takes a little more skill to make. Peel two thin stems of hardwood and then notch the larger one, as shown in B. It should taper a little toward the top, where a groove is cut around it to take the line. After this is done, trim the lower part of the other piece of hardwood, which will be the hook, and carefully whittle it to a long, sharp point. (This is also shown in B.)

The enlarged drawing, C, shows how the point,

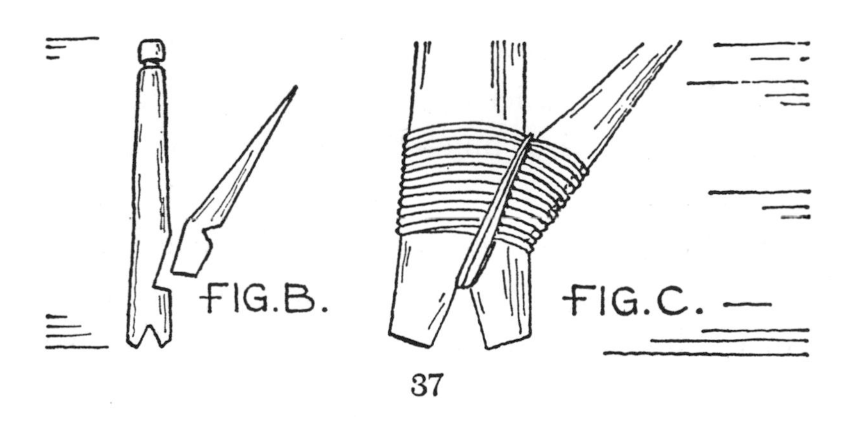

or barb, is fitted and lashed to the notch in the first stem with a cord. To secure the hook firmly and to waterproof it, coat the wrappings with a little pine pitch, if it is available. Simply scrape some into a tin can and set it over the fire to melt. When you use this hook, it must also be baited.

A third hook, which is fashioned from bone, should be made at home before going on a camping or fishing trip. With this method you can make from four to eight hooks at the same time.

When an Iroquois Indian lost one of his bone fishhooks, hours of work were lost with it. His cutting tool was a sharp flake of flint, but you can get the same result by using a scroll saw or a coping saw. He made his hooks from the leg bones of large birds, and you can do the same. The leg bone of a large turkey is just right, as it is hollow and, therefore, easier to work. If you can get one that is uncooked, so much the better, for it will be less brittle.

First of all, mark off the cleaned bone as shown in the dotted lines in figure D. With a coping saw, cut the bone in four pieces, and discard the two end pieces. Saw the two center pieces in half lengthwise. You will now have four sections, shaped like the one in figure E. Into each section drill a hole large enough for the coping-saw blade to pass through. When this is done, cut the center away with the saw, leaving a thin frame, as in F. Then cut the frame into two equal pieces, as in G.

Using a small rattail file for the inner corners and a small flat file for the edges and the point, file the bone pieces down until they look like the

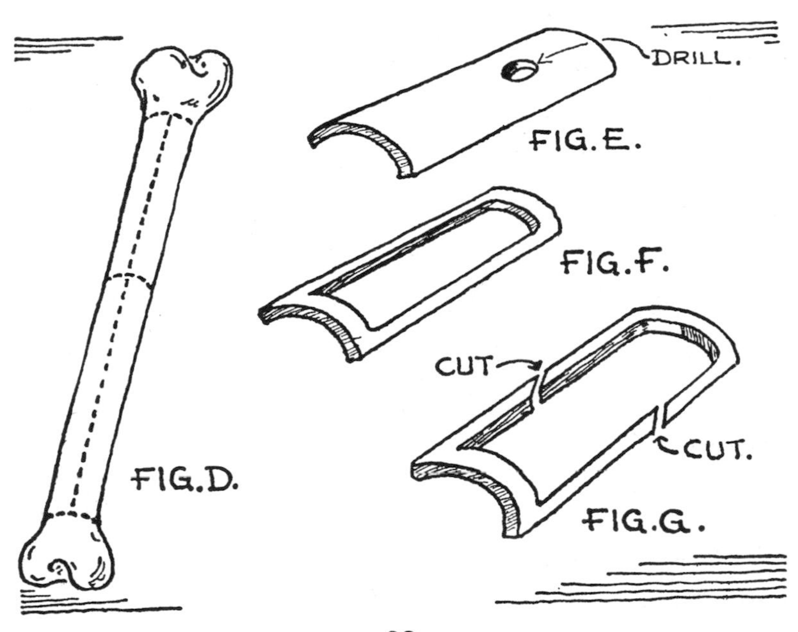

one in figure H. Also file a notch near the top for the line. Now the hook is ready to use. To make the hooks look nice, file all the edges until they are smooth. If you do this work with all four pieces of bone, you will have a supply of eight good bone hooks.

Your father may have a silver spinner in his tackle box, and with very little effort you can make one of your own. Cut a short forked branch, like

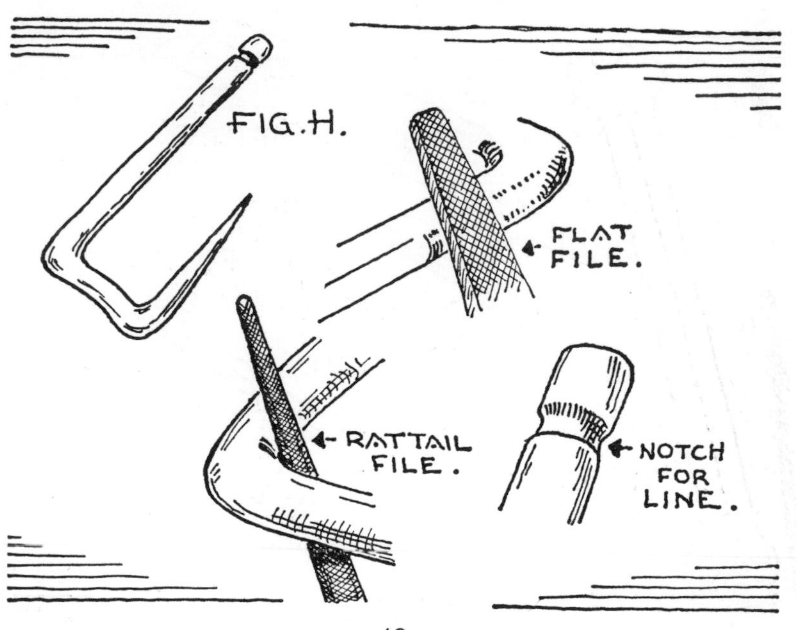

the one shown in I. Peel the bark away down to the white wood underneath. Next, slice off a piece straight down on the left fork, and flatten the other side of the fork in the same manner. Always cut away from you. Trim the top a little with your knife and drill a hole there to pass your line through. Make another hole through the spinner in the V of the crotch. Tie a few strands of colored yarn through it. Strands of hair or small bird feath-

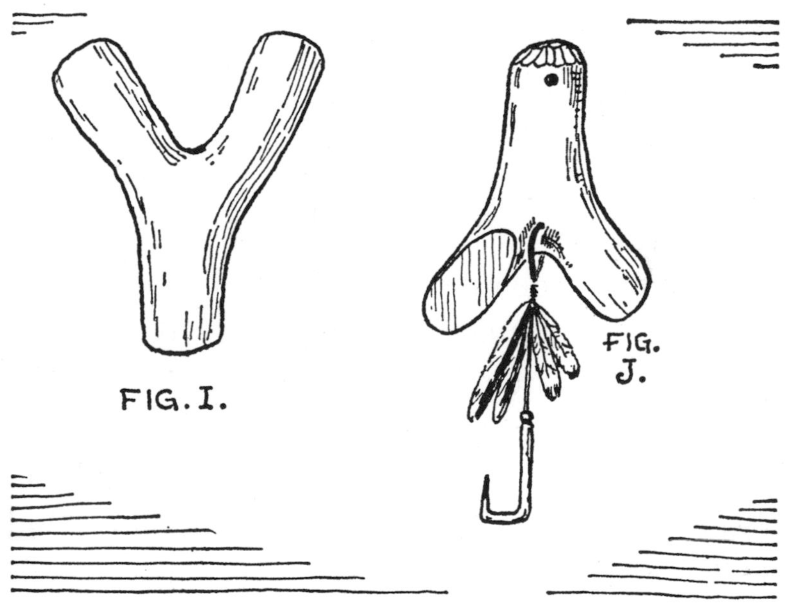

ers can be used instead of the yarn. Tie your fishhook to the same hole. (See J.)

Cast the spinner out on the water as far as possible. When you slowly pull it back toward you, the spinner will flash as it turns and will attract the fish. Lake trout will follow a spinner in the early spring or late fall, but in the summer you must fish deep for them.

If you are still-fishing from a dock or a rock and do not wish to let the hook reach the bottom, you will need a float. You can also find the material for this out-of-doors. Look for a bird feather dropped in flight. Strip the barbs from the quill. Then, with your knife, cut the thick end of the quill at a slant, as in figure K, making the end into a point. Fold, or loop, the point back upon itself, inserting the end into the hollow part of the quill and tying it with a wrapping of fine thread. Pass one end of your fishline through the loop, bring it up to the middle of the quill, and lash it there loosely with some thread. The float should be able to slide up or down the line. (These few steps are illustrated in figure L.)

If you are near a large forest where there are plenty of porcupines, a large quill from one of them will do just as well.

After you have hooked your catch, you may want to land it with a gaff hook. The Indians made theirs from natural material, and so can you. Saplings and forked branches do not always grow in just the right shape near at hand, nor do they all look just like the ones in the drawings. If you scout

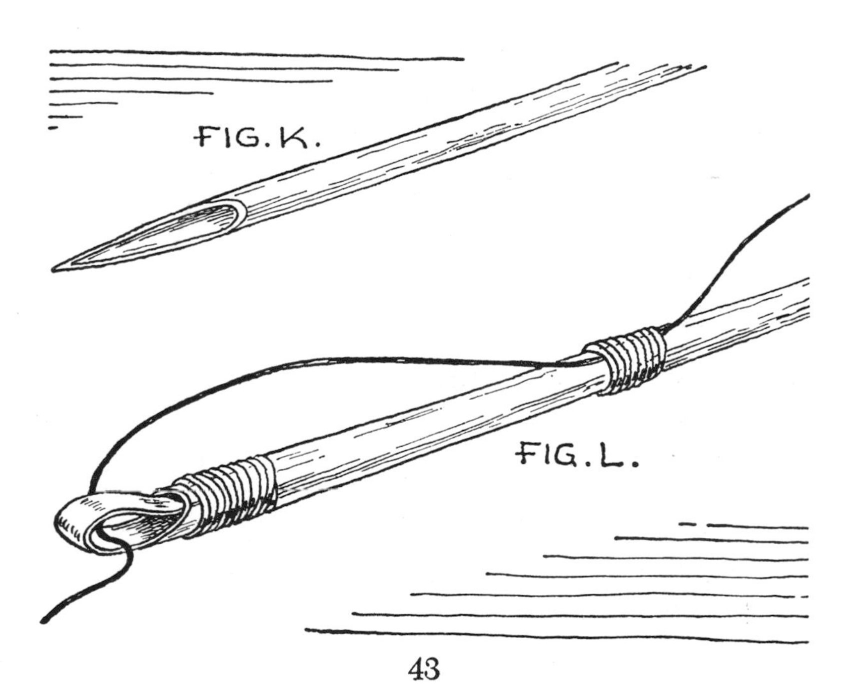

around a bit, however, you can usually find something similar.

First, try to find a young sapling, forked as much as possible like the one in figure M. In that drawing the darkened section is what you will need. Once you have the sapling, cut away all but one of the branches, peel off the bark, and round off the bottom. Then cut the end of the branch in a long, sharp point, as in figure N. The branch will make the hook of your gaff, and the trunk, which need not be more than two feet long, will make the handle. When you have hooked a fish and have played it in close to you, reach down with the gaff hook, insert the point under the gill of the fish, and lift it aboard.

Perhaps you and your father would like to try a little spear fishing. There are two different spears you can make. One is pronged, with a row of nicks cut along the edge of each prong, so that they look like short saws with oversized teeth. The Indians often made this spear from two thin pieces of bone, usually the shinbone of a deer, but it can also be made from hardwood.

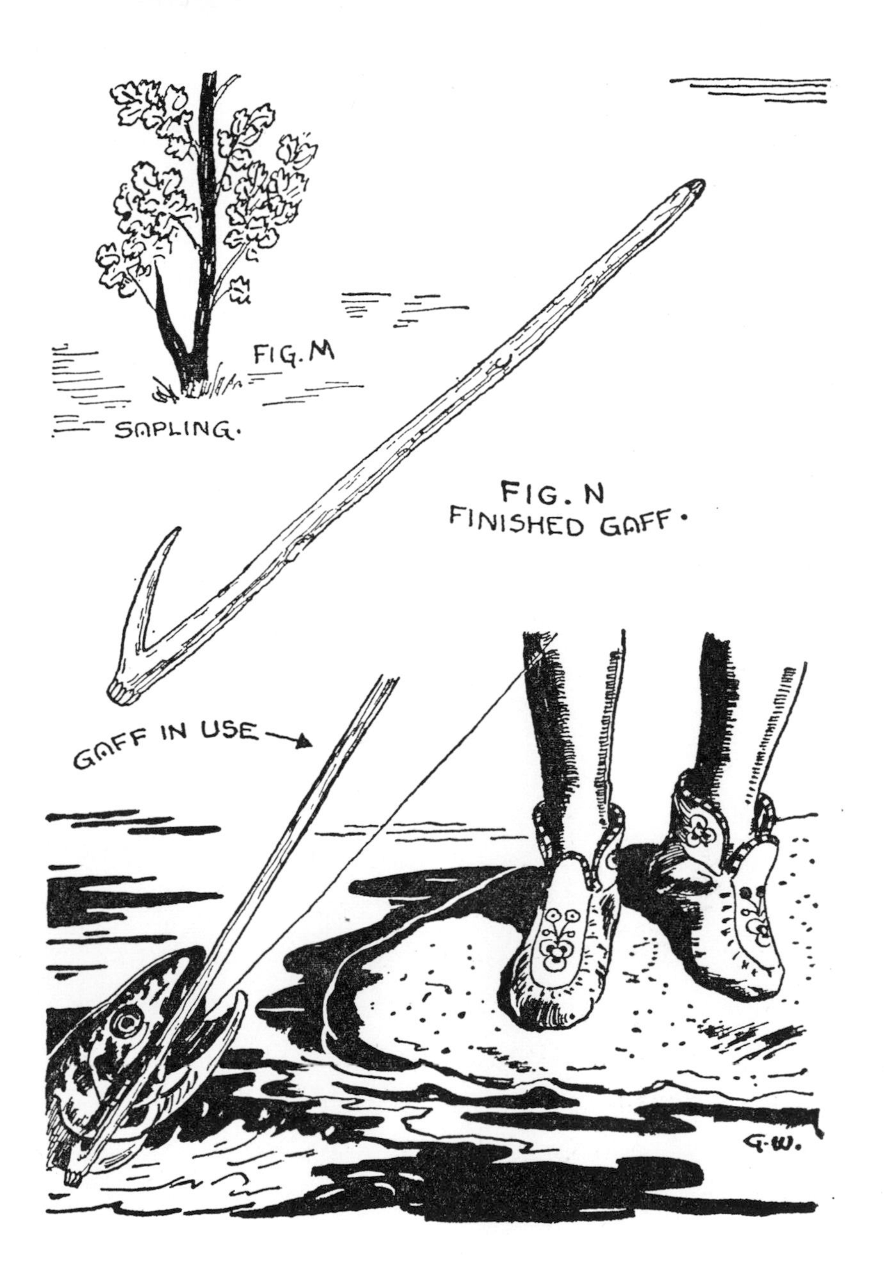
FIG. M
SAPLING.
FIG. N
FINISHED GAFF.
GAFF IN USE
G.W.

Select a hardwood sapling, as straight as possible and from six to seven feet long. Cut it down and carefully peel off the bark. Split the broad end of the sapling down the middle for about eight inches and carefully spread the two pieces apart. To keep them apart, insert a small piece of wood between them. Then, with your knife, start cutting teeth in each piece, as shown in figure O, making sure that they are even and opposite each other. When you have cut five or six teeth along each piece, spread the wood a little more and insert a new wedge in the fork, as shown in the drawing. If pine pitch is available, it can be used as a waterproof glue with which to set the wedge. To keep the stick from splitting, wrap it with basswood bark or strong cord, and then cover it all over with a coating of the pine pitch.

The other spear is a barb type and has a semi-detachable head. It is made most easily from a small deer antler. However, a good hardwood branch of the proper shape can also be used. If you have an antler, grind both points and the stem with a piece of sandstone until they are sharp, as in figure P. If you use wood, whittle it down to the same shape, and whittle the side branch to a point. Cut a handle from a sapling and, after it is peeled, drill a hole in the broad end. Set the longer point of the antler inside the hole, with the shorter point —or barb—facing back toward the handle. The antler should fit loosely enough so that the head can slip out. Next, drill a hole through the antler's long point, pass a cord through it, and knot it. The other end of the cord is then tied to a groove cut in the handle. (See Q.) To prevent the end where the barbed hook is set into the pole from splitting, wrap it with cord. You can protect it even more by holding it with a bone ring. Take a two-inch section of marrow bone—what today is called a soup bone—and clean it out. Then slip it over the shaft from the thin end and push it down tightly over the wide end where the barbed head is attached. If the ring is used, it must be put on before the cord is tied in place.

While the pronged spear is used with a stabbing motion, the barbed spear is thrown. When you strike a fish with it from a canoe, the head of the

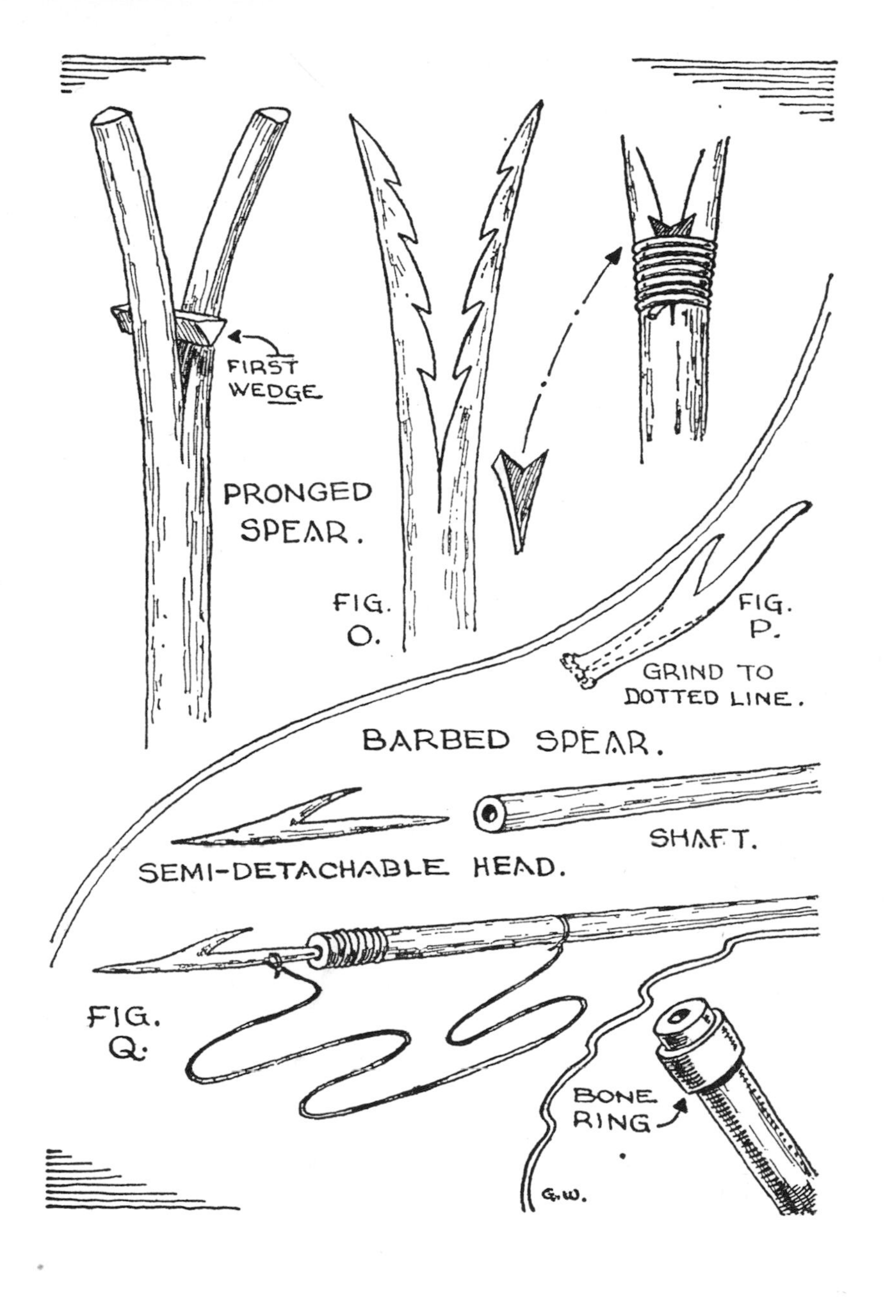
FIRST WEDGE
PRONGED SPEAR.
FIG. O.
FIG. P.
GRIND TO DOTTED LINE.
BARBED SPEAR.
SHAFT.
SEMI-DETACHABLE HEAD.
FIG. Q.
BONE RING
G.W.

spear separates from the shaft. The shaft then floats on the water, where you can easily paddle to it, gather it up, and pull in your catch.

A complete set of these fishing tools, perhaps scaled down to half size, might make an interesting display in your classroom while you are studying the life of the American Indian.

4

Bait Your Hook

WHAT type of bait will the fish take? Most fishermen have their favorites among the artificial flies, both wet and dry, but the fish will also rise to a variety of natural baits. The natural bait you use will depend upon what type of fish you are angling for.

Crickets make a good bait for bass or trout. A hook baited with one need only touch the surface of the water to attract these fish. Trout, bass, perch, and sunfish will also go after the fat, white grub of the May beetle or, in fact, any white grub. This bait is usually found in the decaying mold of a rotting log, and can be dug out with the point of your knife.

Katydids are fine for bass, and grasshoppers are among the best bait for any fish. The fastest way to gather grasshoppers in any numbers is to catch them with a small insect net. Frogs are good for pickerel and bass.

Worms, including the earthworm and the night crawler, have always been good bait. Most of the time bass, trout, eel, perch, sucker, and bullhead are eager to take them. Night crawlers come out of the ground after a rain, and if you sprinkle your lawn in the early evening, you can collect them after dark with a flashlight. Grasp them close to the end nearest their burrow, for at the least disturbance they will vanish back into it.

Minnows, too, make good bait, but they are fast and hard to catch. One good trick is to use a dip net and some bread crumbs. Place the net in the water. Then spread some dry bread crumbs on the surface and wait. When a small group of minnows comes to feed on the bread, bring the net up under them slowly. You can fasten a minnow to your hook without killing or injuring it. If you push the hook through its lower lip and cut through its upper lip, it will swim around freely.

For winter fishing, when most other natural bait is gone or hard to find, the oblong gall growths on the stems of the goldenrod contain grubs that make good bait. In looking over the stems, you will find some of them with small holes on one side. This shows at once that the galls are empty. Those without holes can be cut open along one side to get at the grubs.

There are many more insects and larvae that can be used for fishing, but the ones described here will give you a good start. Good artificial baits include bacon or salt-pork rind and, in a pinch, a shiny piece of fish skin or aluminum foil will do as well.

The fish you land with your baited hook were also caught by the Indians many years ago in much the same areas. On the Pacific Coast the Indians

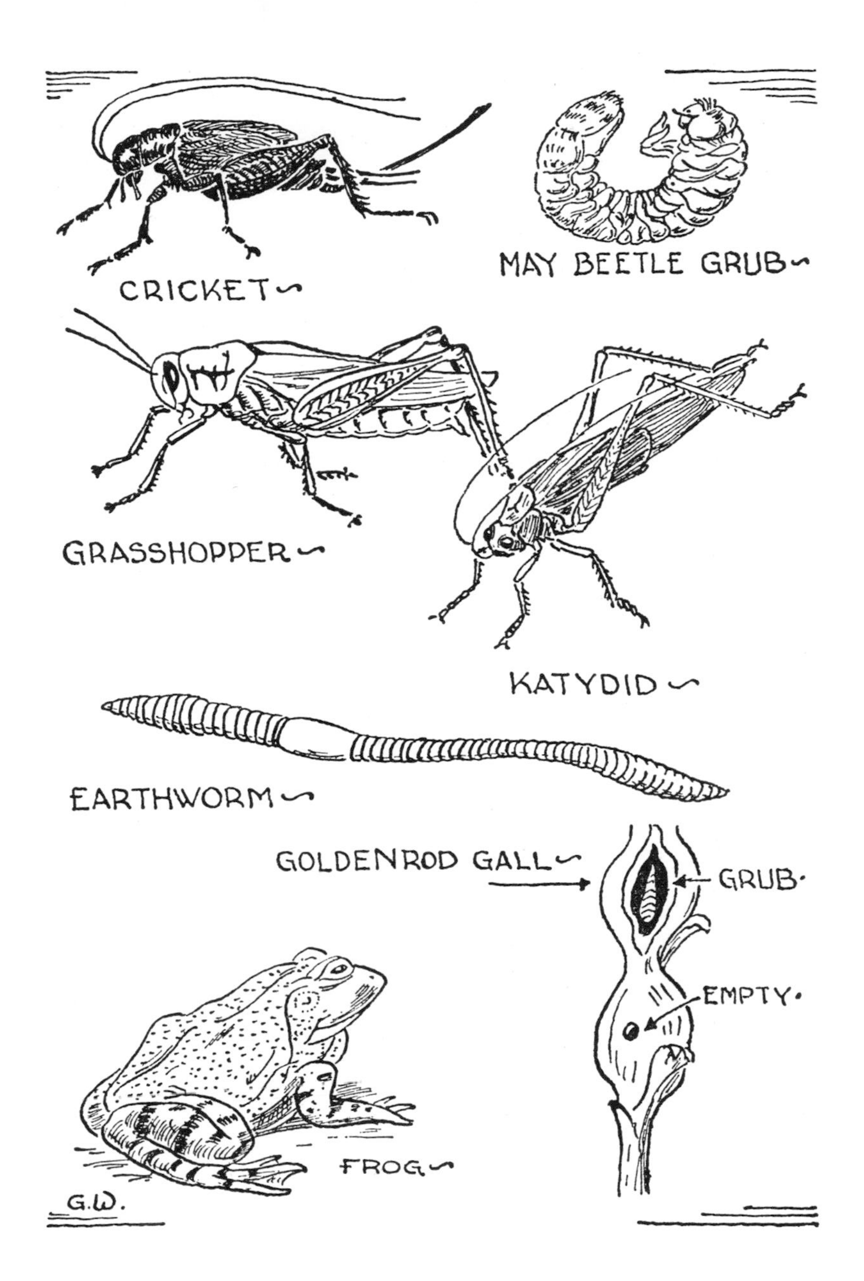
CRICKET
MAY BEETLE GRUB
GRASSHOPPER
KATYDID
EARTHWORM
GOLDENROD GALL
GRUB
EMPTY
FROG
G.W.

fished for salmon. These salmon were the Chinook, sometimes called spring salmon, because in British Columbia they spawn in the late spring. The Chinook are found from southern California north to Alaska and, when full grown, they range in weight from ten to fifty pounds.

These Indians also fished the rivers for candlefish. They belong to the smelt family and are found along the Pacific Coast from Oregon to Alaska. In late winter and early spring their spawning migration brings them in from the sea to the mouths of fresh-water rivers and streams, where the Indians were able to catch them in large quantities. Their oily body, when dried and equipped with a wick, burns like a candle, hence the name candlefish.

The trout belongs to the salmon family, and among those caught by the Indians were the brook trout, the lake trout, the arctic char, and the Dolly Varden. The brook trout is found in lakes, rivers, and brooks, and large ones may weigh up to nine pounds. Lake trout swim in the deep waters of the Great Lakes and also in the larger lakes of Canada. Some weighing eighty-eight pounds have been caught and recorded, but as a rule they come smaller than that. The arctic char can be found in streams emptying into the Arctic Ocean, and eleven pounders are often caught in Hudson Bay. The Dolly Varden, a river fish, runs to a length of thirty-six inches and a weight of twenty pounds.

The whitefish are also related to the salmon. They weigh from two to four pounds and are from twelve to twenty inches long. The whitefish can be found in rivers and bays. Their range extends from Labrador to New England and from the Great Lakes to the Arctic Ocean.

Muskellunge and pickerel both belong to the pike family. The northern pike is strictly a fresh-water fish, reaching a maximum size of four feet. The Great Lakes muskellunge grows to seven feet and weighs over a hundred pounds. Its cousin, the tiger muskellunge, is found in the lakes of Minnesota, Wisconsin, and Ontario, Canada. It is well known to sports fishermen as a fighter.

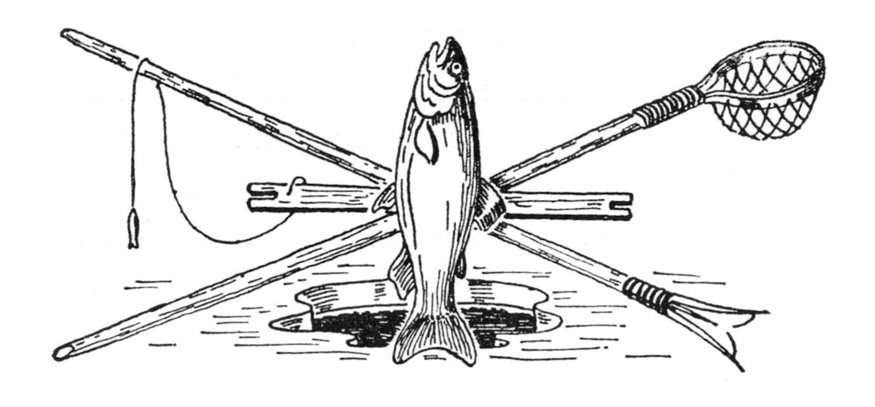

5

Winter Fishing

FISHING is not restricted to any particular month of the year. You can enjoy this sport even in the winter. Fishing through the ice has been known to the Eskimo for centuries, and it is done today in many parts of the United States, especially along the Canadian border.

In the treeless arctic the winters are long, and the summers are so short that even the hardiest berries often fail to ripen fully. The rivers and inlets, even large portions of the sea, are frozen over during nine months of the year. Even so, fishing provided much of the Eskimo's food. He caught trout, whitefish, and salmon through holes cut in the ice and through the natural cracks that formed in the ice close to shore. Such fishing called for a great deal of skill and patience. When the fish ran in plenty, it did not take a man long to catch more than he needed. On days when the fish had taken to deeper waters, the fisherman often tried one hole after another and, at the end of the day, arrived home with only one or two small fish, or even with none at all.

Fishing through the ice also had its elements of danger, especially when it was done far from shore. A sudden change of wind or a sudden rise in temperature might cause large ice floes to break away. If this happened while a fisherman was intent upon his work, it was not uncommon for him to drift out into open water, and no one ever saw him again.

An ice fisherman had to disregard the icy winds that constantly swept over him. To protect himself from them at his fishing hole, the Eskimo at times put up a shelter. Such a shelter was usually nothing more than a large animal hide hung over a tripod made from driftwood. In addition to sheltering him a little, it also gave him a dark interior, which helped him to see deeper into the water.

Other Indians also used similar shelters, and the European settlers soon adopted the idea. When ice fishing became a sport, people began building better shelters. They now have a floor, raised off the ice, with a hole in it that can be covered with a trap door. The shelter is built without windows, and the fisherman usually furnishes it with a small stove for warmth and for boiling coffee.

Sheltered or not, the ice fisherman still has a two-handed job. He must hold his line and lure in one hand and the spear in his other. At the moment the fish comes to the lure, he must strike fast and spear it. This is the thrill of the game.

The Eskimo used an entirely different type of fishing gear from that of other Indians. Yet it is not hard to duplicate it today, except for one or two items that are difficult for us to obtain. We can substitute for them and still get the same results.

You will need a rod, line, lure, a small ice scoop, a fish spear, and a hook.

The Eskimo usually made his fishing rod from a piece of driftwood fourteen inches long. Whittled to a flat shape, it had a deep notch cut into each end. At one end the fishing line was fastened. When not in use, the line was wound around the rod lengthwise, with the notches holding it in place.

The fishline was made of whale bone. This type of bone did not come from the skeleton of the whale, but from the flexible, comblike baleen strip, which is the food strainer found in the mouth of the toothless blue whale and the right whale. The baleen was split into very fine strands, which never kinked. When ice formed on the wet line, a quick shake snapped it off.

Onto the free end of the line the Eskimo tied a small jigger, or lure, carved from a piece of bone or ivory. These pieces usually represented very small fish or, most often, shrimp. You can substitute cord or fishline for the baleen strip and lead for the ivory.

GRAY-
WOLF.

The scoop net was very important. With it the Eskimo fisherman scooped loose pieces of ice out of his fishing hole. It was also used to keep the hole open, for in the cold air new ice formed rapidly over the open water. The net, too, was made from baleen strips. The hoop from which the net hung was formed from a sliver of moose antler that had been boiled in water until pliable and then bent into shape. The baleen strips were passed through holes drilled in the hoop, and then tied into a shallow net. The hoop was fastened firmly to a wooden handle, which was anywhere from two to five feet long.

In the winter these scoops were carried everywhere by the villagers, and although they had been designed for one purpose originally, the Eskimo boys invented a new use for them. They became quite expert at picking up a scoopful of snow and throwing it with a great deal of force and accuracy at any chosen target.

An equally useful article was the spear. It had a shaft about twenty inches long with three prongs, made of bone, firmly set into one end of it. The middle prong was straight and about four inches long. A nine-inch prong came out at an angle on each side of it. Holes were drilled near the points of the two outside prongs, and into each of these a flexible prong, or spur, was set so that it pointed inward and upward toward the middle prong. When a fish was attracted to the lure dangling just below the water line, the Eskimo struck down quickly with the poised spear. This quick thrust impaled the fish on the center prong. If it was a small fish the flexible spurs below it on the outside prongs prevented it from slipping off when the spear was drawn out of the water.

Spears of this type are still used today, and although the prongs are now made of metal, the shape has changed very little. Should you be interested in making and using such a spear, substitute carefully whittled pieces of hardwood for the bone the Eskimos used. Step by step directions for construction are given on the opposite page.

The Eskimos ice fished with a single baited copper hook or with a four-pronged ivory jigger. These were the earliest, pre-European fishhooks,

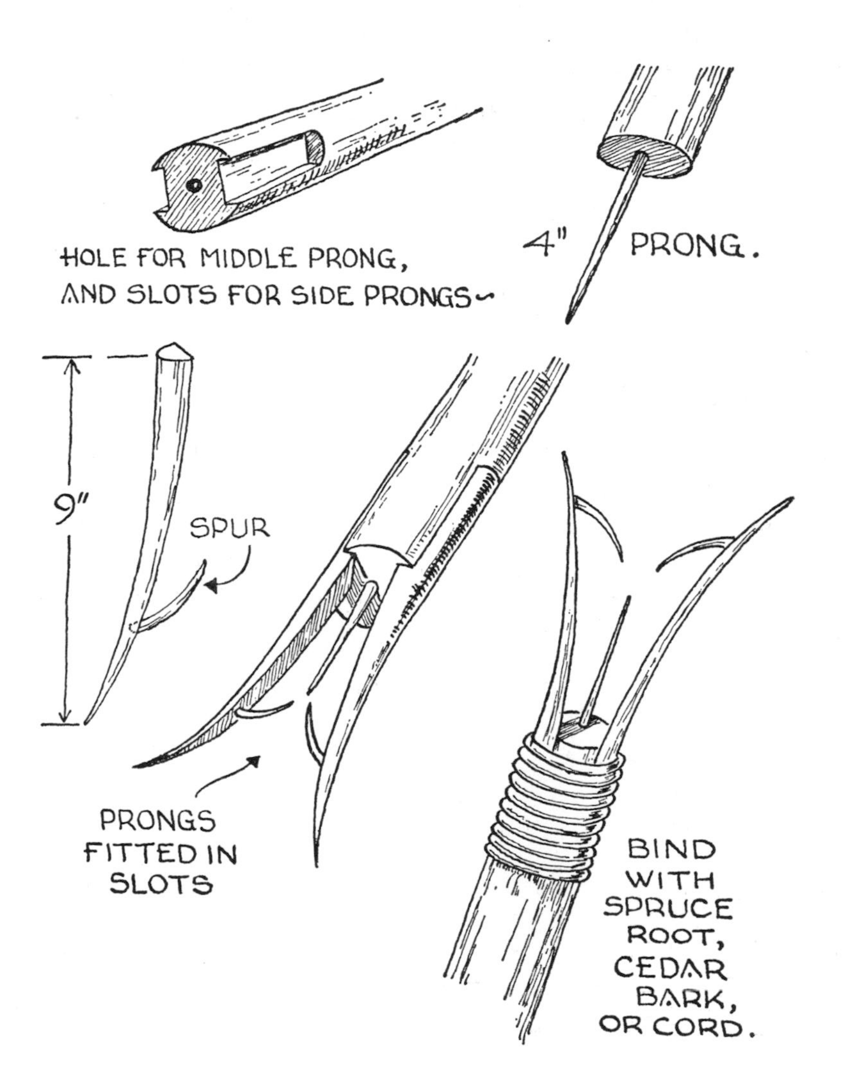

~THE THREE-PRONGED SPEAR~

and they were made without barbs from copper found on the surface of the ground or in veins in the earth. An Eskimo bent up a thin piece of copper to form a hook, which was a little broader at the bottom than at the top. He attached this hook to one side of a flat piece of antler bone, which had a hole drilled at the top to take the line.

The four-pronged jigger was carved from a piece of walrus ivory, in a shape resembling a

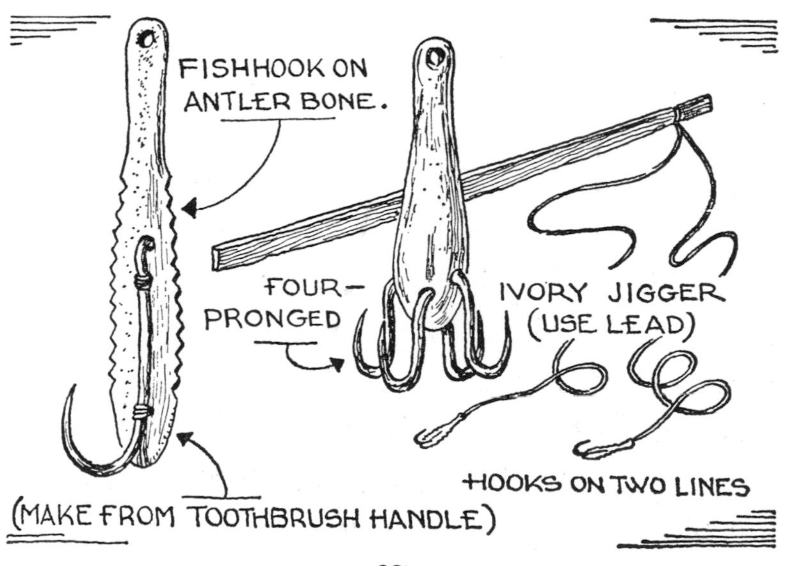

small club. At the top of it, a hole was drilled to take the fishline. Two more holes were drilled all the way through the broad end, so that they crossed, one above the other, in the middle. Through these holes two copper strands were passed and their ends bent into barbless hooks. The club end of the ivory jigger then had four hooks hanging around it.

A barbless hook was necessary in the arctic. In that cold climate a fish froze solid almost the instant it was brought out of the water. When an Eskimo caught a fish on his barbless hook, he could dislodge it with a deft jerk without removing his mittens, so his hands remained perfectly dry.

The Eskimo also never touched his wet fishline, even when he pulled it in. Holding the short fishing rod in one hand and his ice scoop in the other, he lifted part of the line with the scoop, the next part with the rod. He alternated between the scoop and the rod, crisscrossing, until he had wound up the entire line and had pulled the fish out of the hole onto the ice.

GRAY-
WOLF.

One fish the Eskimos caught in warmer weather was the salmon. During the summer, when the salmon migration was on and they passed through the shallow arctic streams to spawn, the Eskimo fishermen blocked their way with large boulders. As the fish darted about in an effort to reach open water, they walked among them and speared them by the hundreds.

6

Cook Your Catch

THE flesh of a fish tastes better if it is killed as soon as it is taken from the water, and for this purpose most Indians carried a short hardwood club. Many anglers of today keep a combination knife and fish club in their tackle box.

Another good idea is to clean your fish as soon as possible, for this also improves the taste. If you are on a canoe trip, there is no better place for cleaning your fish than on the flat blade of your paddle. Placed on a level spot on the ground, it makes a fine worktable. To prepare a fish for eating, start by cutting out the backbone fin. This is done by cutting on both sides of it and then pulling it forward and out. Remove the other fins in the same way. The next step is to slit the belly of the fish and remove the intestines. Finally cut off the head just back of the gills.

If you are fishing in muddy water or in a swamp, the catch should be skinned in order to remove the muddy taste. First remove the backbone fin and cut the belly. Make a cut behind the gills joining the backbone and belly cuts. Then rip off the skin on each side. If you cut around the head carefully and not all the way through, you will be able to remove the head and the intestines at the same time.

Fish that isn't skinned should be scaled. When scaling a fish, scrape it from tail to head, keeping the scales wet while you work. Brook trout, however, are smooth, and need only be washed off.

Last of all, wash the inside of the fish with cold

water to remove all blood, and dry it with a cloth or towel.

In handling any kind of fish you will get odors on your hands. They can be removed by washing your hands with salt and hot water. After you have rinsed them well, wash them again in more hot water, using plenty of soap. But be sure to use the salt first.

Frying is the fastest, easiest, and most popular way to cook fish. If they are small, they can be fried whole, but a large fish should be cut up. Beat an egg in a rather flat pan, dip the fish in it, and then roll the fish in flour or corn meal. Salt and pepper it well and fry it in corn oil or bacon grease. The fat should be about a quarter of an inch deep in the skillet, and it should be hot, although not hot enough to smoke. Brown the fish on both sides, watching it closely, as it only takes from three to five minutes to cook it through.

Without a frying pan, you can cook your catch with the aid of green sticks. *Green* means the condition of the wood, not the color. If wood bends, it is green and will not burn. Therefore, it can be

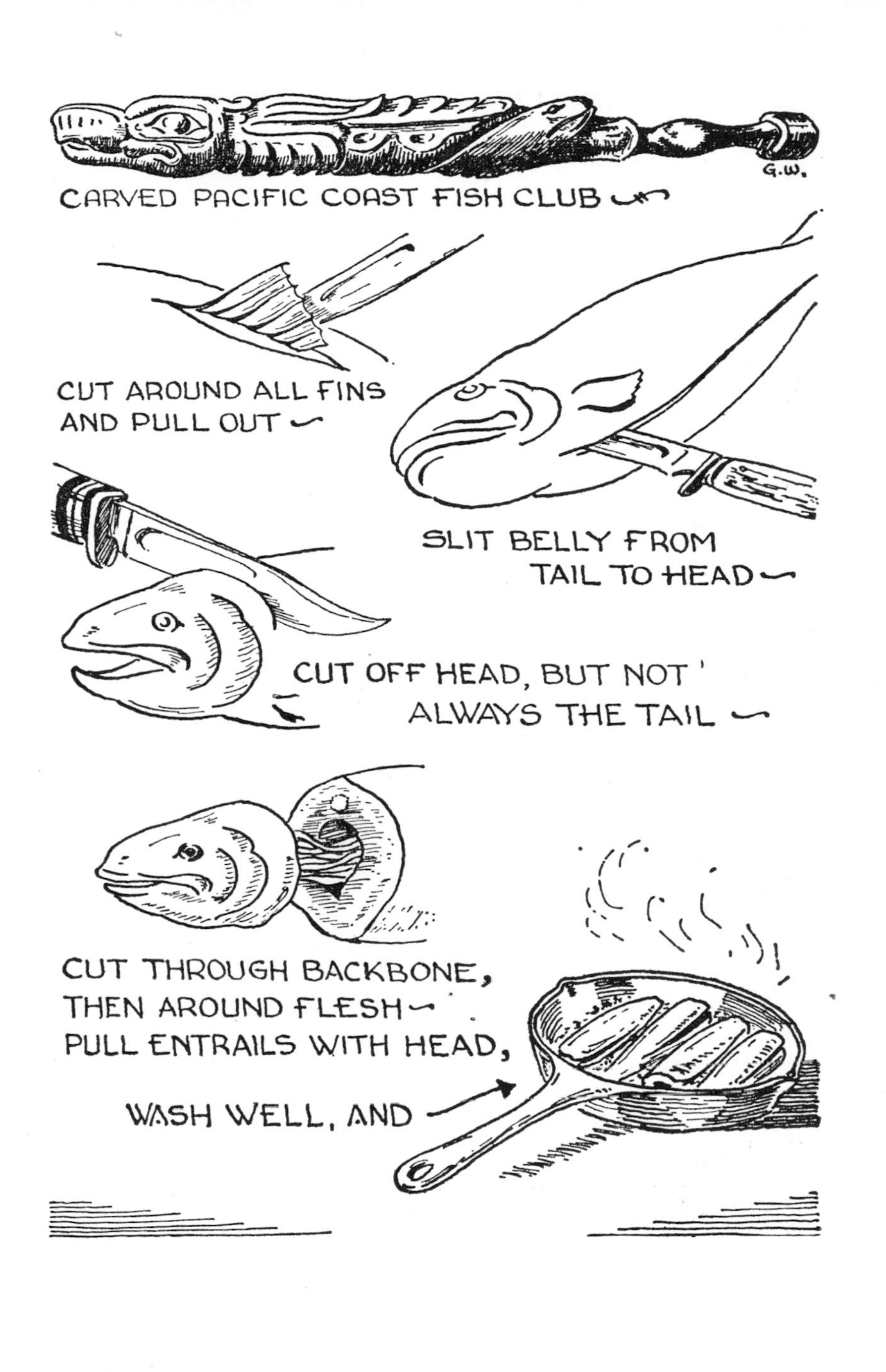
G.W.
CARVED PACIFIC COAST FISH CLUB
CUT AROUND ALL FINS
AND PULL OUT
SLIT BELLY FROM
TAIL TO HEAD
CUT OFF HEAD, BUT NOT
ALWAYS THE TAIL
CUT THROUGH BACKBONE,
THEN AROUND FLESH
PULL ENTRAILS WITH HEAD,
WASH WELL, AND

used close to the heat. Wood that snaps or breaks should be used for firewood.

When preparing a fish for the green-stick method, cut off its head, but leave the tail attached. Split the fish open right down to the tail and clean well. Select a green stick twenty-five to thirty inches long, peel off the bark, and then insert it into the fish from neck to tail. Another green stick, just long enough to spread the sides of the fish apart, is placed inside the fish so that the two sticks form a cross. If you wish, you can tie this cross together with a short cord or a strand of bark fiber. When cooking large fish use two cross sticks.

When you have a stick that is long enough, you can sit by the hot coals and hold the fish over them. You can also rest the stick on a rock, holding the end in place with a cut branch, as shown on page 81. In either case, the fish should be turned from time to time.

Another way to prepare fish without cooking utensils is by planking it. Again leave the tail on the fish. Then spread it open and, with short wooden pegs, tack it to the flat side of a slab of softwood. Use the flat side of your ax blade, which is called the butt, or poll, as a hammer for tapping in the pegs. Then cut a strong stick, and use it to prop the slab up in front of a good hot fire, or sit it up in front of a reflector fire.

Cooking in aluminum foil is a good way to prepare fish. After it has been cleaned, wrap a couple of strips of bacon around it and place it in the foil. Close all the openings in the foil and cover the package with hot coals. It takes from twelve to twenty-five minutes to cook, depending on the size of the fish.

Aluminum-foil cookery is, of course, a modern method, but flat-stone cookery was invented by the Indians. After finding a large flat stone, brush it and wash it well. Then make sure it is well dried before using it. Raise it off the ground on four stones of fairly equal size and build a hot fire underneath it. To find out whether the slab is hot enough, drop a little water on it. If the water sizzles as it touches the stone, the slab is ready. Once the stone is hot, keep the fire going to supply

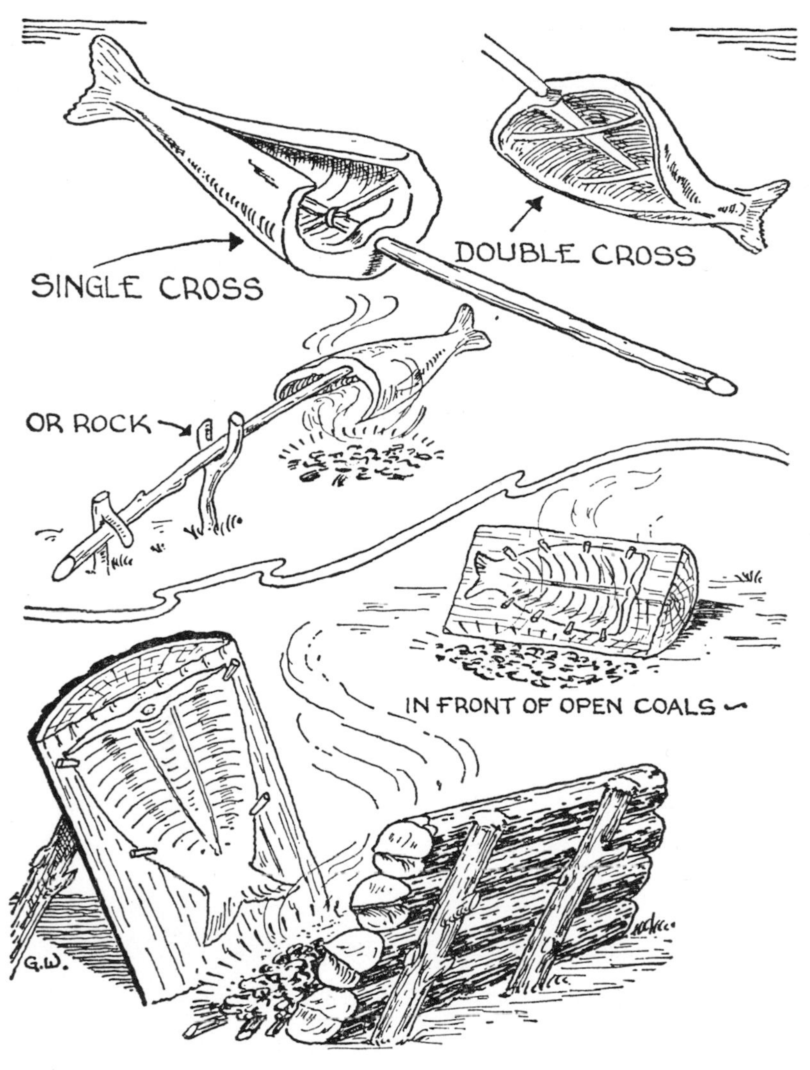
DOUBLE CROSS
SINGLE CROSS
OR ROCK
IN FRONT OF OPEN COALS
G.W.
IN FRONT OF REFLECTOR FIRE

a steady amount of heat for as long as you need to cook your meal.

If you are in a so-called stand camp—that is, if the camp is to remain there for the full vacation—then it will be worth your while to prepare the stone more carefully. When it first starts to get hot, rub it with either a piece of suet or with a slab of bacon rind. This will prevent the food from

sticking. In either case, meat, fish, griddle cakes, and eggs can be cooked on the hot slab.

One good way to keep an egg from spreading after you break the shell is to take a slice of bread, tear out a part of its center, and place the bread on the slab. The heat will bind it to the stone, and you simply break the egg within the hole. This holds the egg together, and in the end you have a fried egg with a slice of toast.

Mud is another good cooking aid, and when you use it to cook fish, you do not need to scale the fish first. Just cut it open, clean it well, and cut off the head and tail. Roll out or pat mud or clay, which you can find beside a stream, into the shape of a large dinner plate. Place the fish near the center of it and fold over the sides, so that the fish is completely covered. Place this in the fire and cover it with hot coals. The length of time for baking will depend upon the size of the fish. Once it is taken out of the fire and the clay or mud is cracked open, the skin comes off with the clay, and the fish is clean and well done.

If you have luck and catch too many fish to eat

at one meal, you can dry the fish that are left over. Split them down the back and remove the backbone and the entrails. Then, after the fish have been thoroughly washed, hang them on a rack to dry in the sun and air. Fish that have been dried to a crisp have a wonderful taste when broiled on a rack over a bed of hot coals.

When you are fishing by a lake that has a nice sandy beach, you can bury your catch in the cool, wet sand, and it will keep until you are ready to go back to camp. But be sure to mark the spot, so that if you wander away you can find it again.

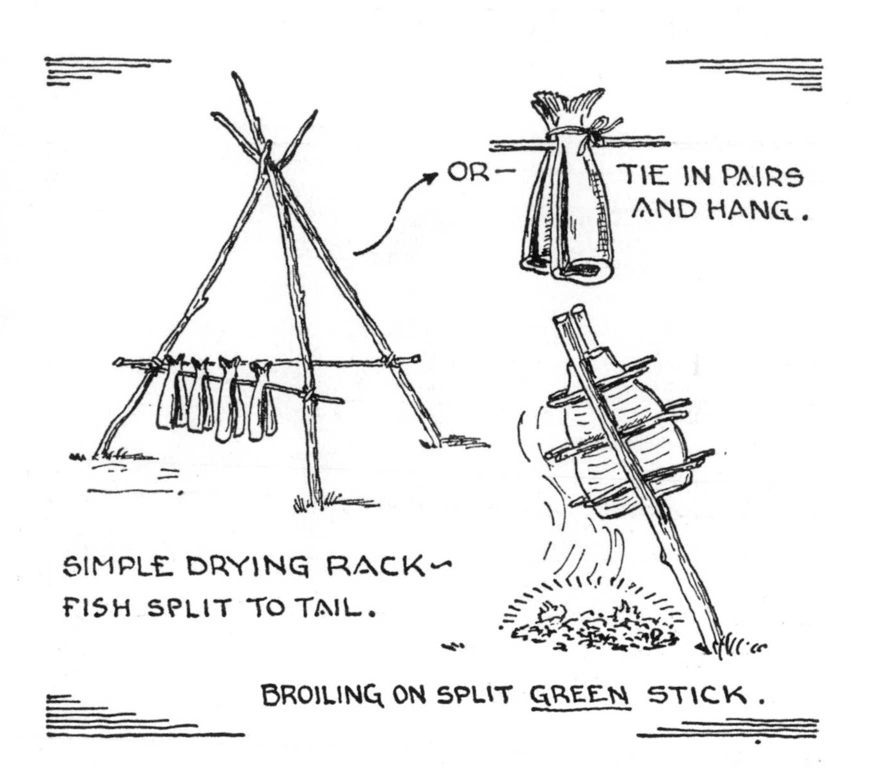

7

Safety on the Trail

WANDERING away from camp, especially in strange territory, can be dangerous. An old story tells about two hunters who were looking for their camp. They met an Indian, rushed up to him, and told him they were lost. He replied, "You're not lost. You're here. Your tepee's lost!" However, whether it is you or your camp that is lost makes little difference.

Many things can be done beforehand to prevent this from happening to you. First of all, know where you are going by using a map. The road maps offered at many filling stations are useful when you wish to find out what highways to take from one place to another, but for camping and exploring the best maps you can get are the government topographical maps. They are printed in sections, so that you can send for only the ones that cover the country in which you plan to camp.

Naturally you and your family do not expect to get lost, but it is always best to know what to do in an emergency. Mark off on your map the spot where you leave the main road, the dirt road you follow from there, and the trail, if you have to go in to your camp by foot. When you have reached your camp spot, mark it on the map too.

You will most likely camp near a stream, river, or lake. If it is a stream or river, check with your compass to see in which direction the water flows, and make a note of this. Any trails listed that you may later explore should also be marked on the map. Then, if the trail leads north away from camp, you will know that you will have to travel south by the compass to get back again.

GROVE
U.P.R.R.
TRAIL
106
CAMP
HIGHLAND
TOMAHAWK LAKE
TOTEM HILL
900
BASS LAKE
GRAY-WOLF.

The best way to do this marking is to spread the map open and check with the compass until the compass needle and the line marked "North" on the map both point in the same direction. You can then place the compass on the map and, from its points, mark off the directions of all the trails you plan to follow during your camping trip.

If you have a good compass, *never* argue with it. Even though you may feel you are heading in the wrong direction, remember that while you have been traveling, the sun has been moving across the sky, which may confuse your sense of direction.

When you use a compass, never place it near any metal, such as your ax or hunting knife, because the needle will be drawn toward the metal instead of toward the magnetic north.

Whenever you leave camp alone, always make sure that those remaining in camp have a general idea of where you are going. Then go there, and don't change your mind as you travel along. You will probably not lose the trail if you have studied it well but, in case you do, remember to stay where you are. If you don't return to camp at the time you said you would, someone will come to look for you.

Perhaps on an earlier trip you made some of the Indian fishing gear described in this book. If you ever become lost and have nothing with you but the hunting knife on your belt, this knowledge will help you to find food. You can make a thin bark line stripped from a young sapling, a gorge hook, and a gaff. With a little luck, you will then be able to catch fish.

But one more word of warning. Whenever you go on a fishing trip, check first with the local Fish and Game Warden to see what equipment is legal in his state or county. In some places, spear fishing, for example, is not permitted, and torchlight fishing is against the law in all states.

However, making and using the old tools of the Indian will give you a lot of enjoyment, and will add to your knowledge of the out-of-doors.

ATLANTIC SALMON
CHINOOK SALMON
WHITEFISH
AMERICAN SMELT (CANDLEFISH)
G.W.

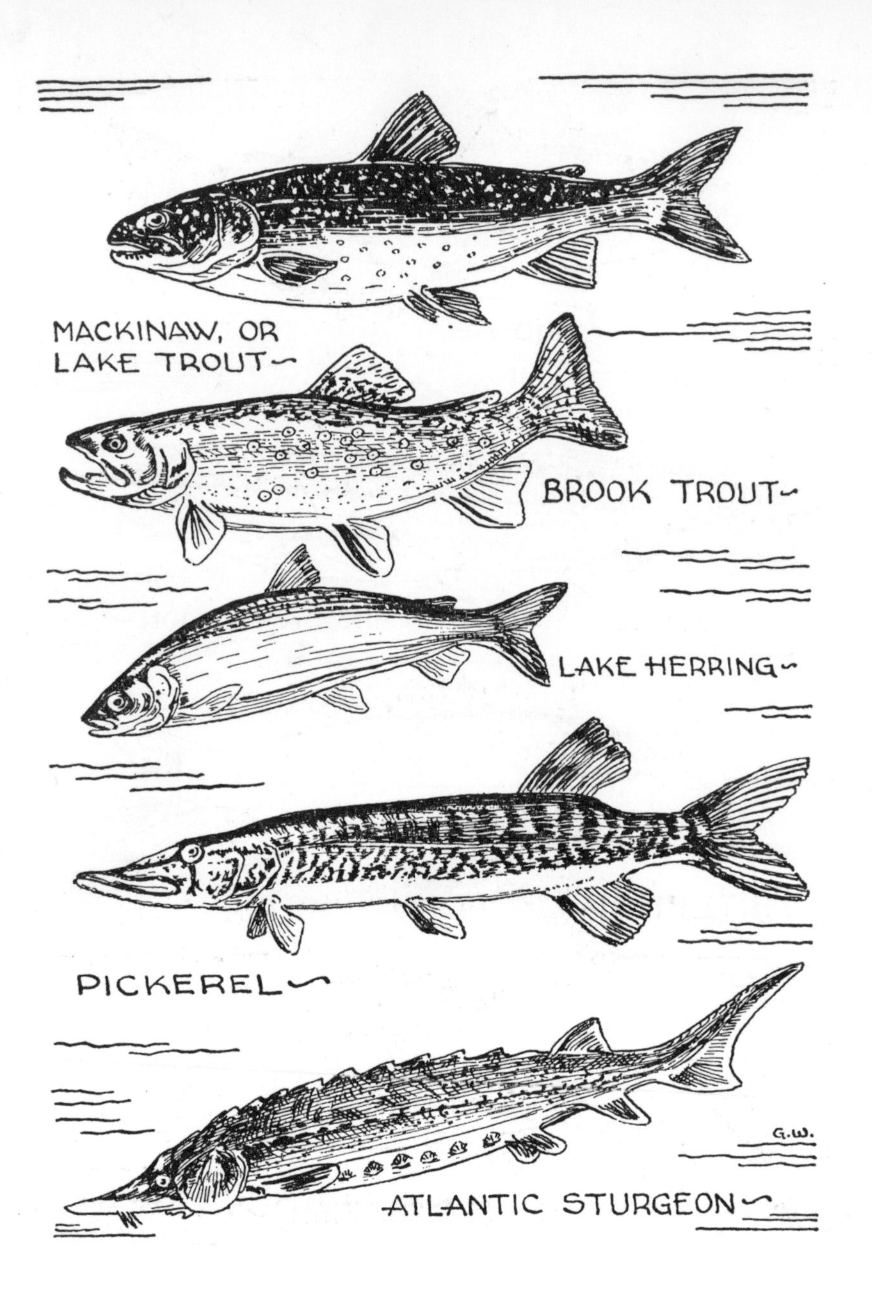
MACKINAW, OR
LAKE TROUT
BROOK TROUT
LAKE HERRING
PICKEREL
G.W.
ATLANTIC STURGEON

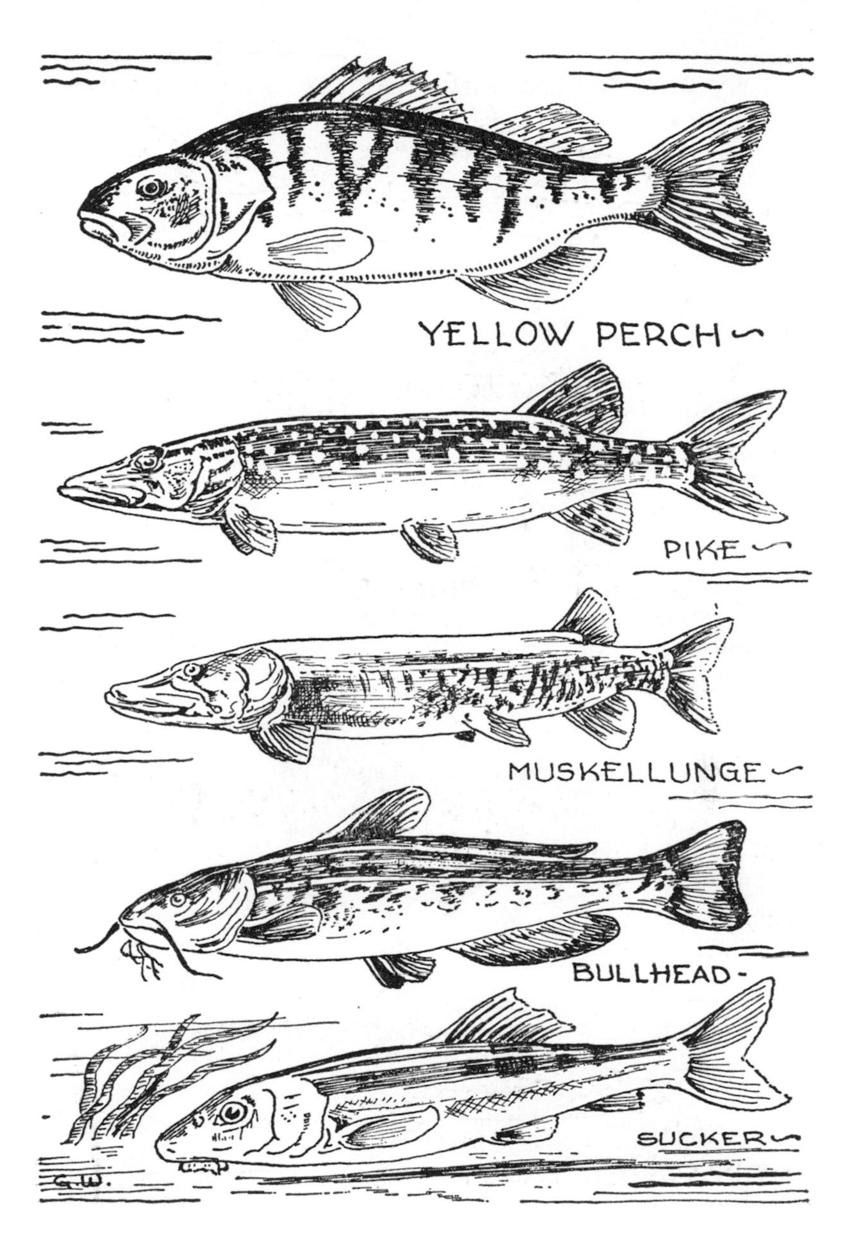
YELLOW PERCH
PIKE
MUSKELLUNGE
BULLHEAD
SUCKER
G.W.

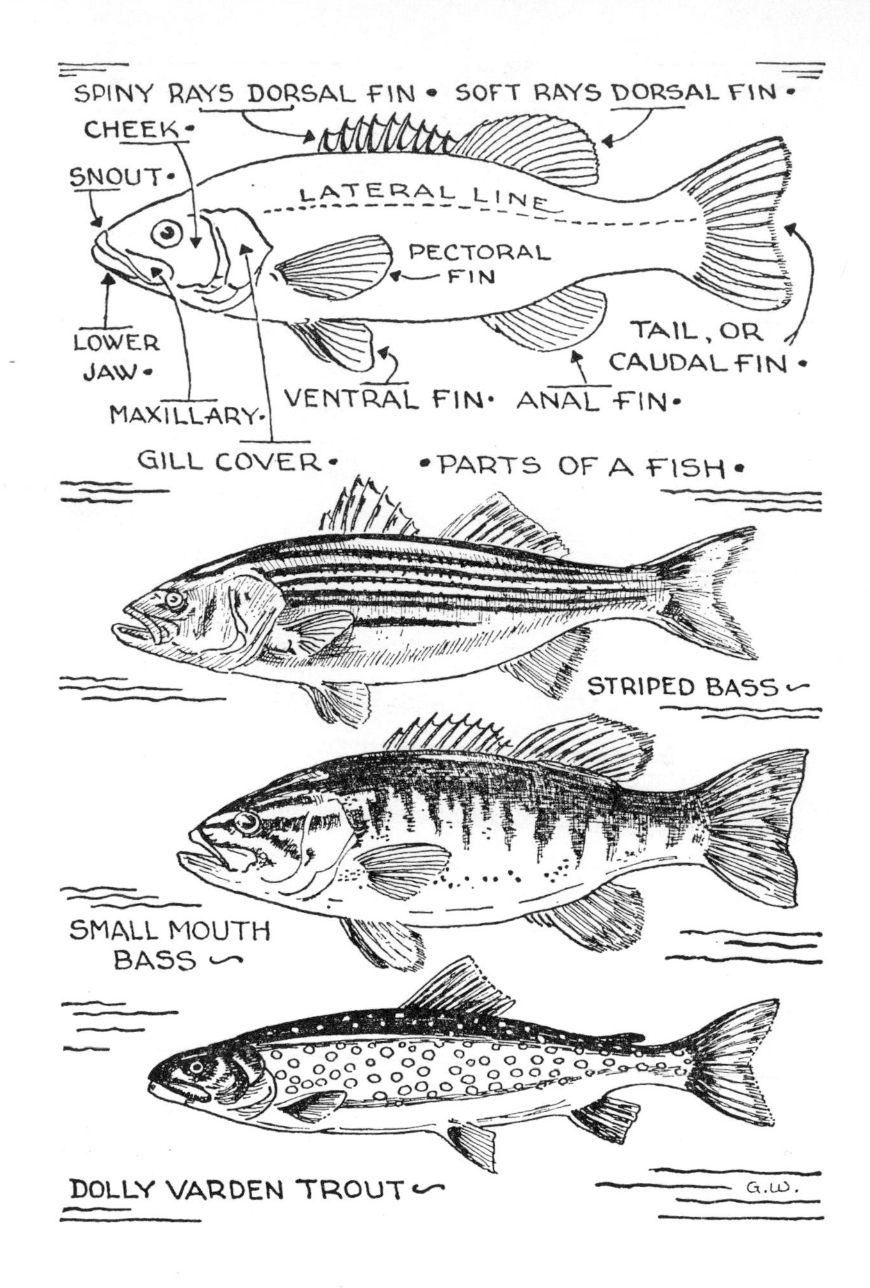
SPINY RAYS DORSAL FIN •
SOFT RAYS DORSAL FIN •
CHEEK •
SNOUT •
LATERAL LINE
PECTORAL FIN
LOWER JAW •
MAXILLARY •
GILL COVER •
VENTRAL FIN •
ANAL FIN •
TAIL, OR CAUDAL FIN •
• PARTS OF A FISH •
STRIPED BASS
SMALL MOUTH BASS
DOLLY VARDEN TROUT
G.W.